THE CHAIR (

JE

By the same author

The Cost of Seriousness (1978, reissued 1987)
Fast Forward (1984)
The Automatic Oracle (1987)
Collected Poems (1983, reissued 1988)
A Porter Selected (1989)
Possible Worlds (1989)

THE CHAIR
OF BABEL

Peter Porter

Oxford   Melbourne
OXFORD UNIVERSITY PRESS
1992

Oxford University Press, Walton Street, Oxford OX2 6DP

Oxford New York Toronto
Delhi Bombay Calcutta Madras Karachi
Petaling Jaya Singapore Hong Kong Tokyo
Nairobi Dar es Salaam Cape Town
Melbourne Auckland
and associated companies in
Berlin Ibadan

Oxford is a trade mark of Oxford University Press

First published in Oxford Poets
as an Oxford University Press paperback 1992

British Library Cataloguing in Publication Data
Data available

Library of Congress Cataloging in Publication Data
Porter, Peter.
The chair of Babel / Peter Porter.
p.   cm. — (Oxford poets)
I. Title. II. Series.
PR9619.3.P57C48   1992   821 — dc20   91-23563
ISBN 0-19-282920-3

Typeset by Wyvern Typesetting Ltd.
Printed in Hong Kong

For my granddaughters,
Amelia and Martha

ACKNOWLEDGEMENTS

Acknowledgements are due to the editors of the following periodicals in which some of these poems first appeared: *Acumen*, *Adelaide Review*, *Agenda*, *Ambit*, *Encounter*, *English Literature in Translation*, *New Statesman*, *Orbis*, *Overland*, *Poetry Book Society Christmas Supplement 1989*, *The Rialto*, *Soho Square* (1989), *Spokes*, *Staple*, *Strawberry Fare*, *Thames Poetry*, *The Times Literary Supplement*, *Verse*. One poem was included in 'Robert Graecen at Seventy' (*Poetry Ireland*), and one in the Festschrift for Raymond Tschumi (Hochschule, St Gallen, Switzerland). 'A Tale of Two Pieties' was specially commissioned by BBC Television.

My gratitude goes to the Trustees of Hawthornden Castle, Lothian, for giving me a resident Fellowship in 1990, where several of the poems in this book were written.

CONTENTS

A YES AND A NO

A Yes includes a No the body says,
absorbed in its unhappiness,
and music will not let the ears forget
that 'saved again' sounds very like 'as yet',
the old placebo of a guess

No wonder rapists hear a No as Yes.
Repentance tastes like *Punt e Mes*.
The fleet is still at sea; the ports regret
their one-time empire, all its rudders wet,
       now Yes includes a No.

Every cruel commandment more or less
will find its sacrificial Tess
and poetry from ode to triolet   .
can alter nothing, merely put its 'stet'
on each unfairness, pleased enough to stress
       that Yes includes a No.

THE CHILD AT SIXTY

The harpsichord plays out of black or silver grooves
And undulant air receives the message of
A past where with the rhythm of hard hooves
Each inexorable part of you vibrates
At memories of gardens, faces, loves,
The hiding behind doors, the padlocked gates
And backs of friends, the well-invested hates.

Such fear and palsy in the grey will then compel
The greedy child to claw back sixty years
And find himself along the path from hell
He missed first time, and being old but now
Replete with charm and cunning trim his fears
With bright armorial lies and mutter how
What time condemns the music will allow.

ENCOURAGEMENT TO SLEEP

The things beside the bed will wake with you.
   To wake with you your mind must live through sleep.
Alive through sleep your dream keeps you in view.
   What dreams can view will not be yours to keep.
What's yours to keep is all the world ahead.
The world ahead is things beside the bed.

And there you enter when you close your eyes.
   Unclose your eyes and see what time has made.
Time has made a tomb from its supplies
   Since it supplies such brilliance as will fade.
Such as will fade is brilliant at the centre.
Things at the centre touch and there you enter.

GO SOME OF YOU, AND FETCH A LOOKING-GLASS

When Hardy looked into his glass he saw
A younger self of real not ghostly pain
And knew the travelling law
That youthful loss is framed as adult gain.

The reader reads and thinks he understands:
He's still inside the huge machine which time
Put in his parents' hands
And staved on paper with confirming rhyme.

They are themselves and so they can't be him,
And somewhere as his ancestors retreat
Intrusive Cherubim
Make singular the general defeat.

Always the present lingers in the glass.
The lawn is mown and soon the daisies rise
Above the new-mown grass
And looking in the mirror blanks the eyes.

NOTHING NEITHER WAY

I saw the world cease at my cradle's foot.
Beginning life with knowledge of its end
I wasn't told what acts would come between.

I meant to be a writer who put down
the truth dressed in its absolute brown clothes
but found myself in motley in my dreams.

I learned to live with my contending powers
and feel the warmth of being what I was
the while my species swarmed beneath the sun.

Natural History Programmes pictured mice
alive beneath the desert sand, clusters
of ants like music's notes on wide patrol.

And all the while a silent ticking told
my individual fate, my siege of self,
I was the screen where history would show.

'War declared today, went for a swim',
'got my *Zauberflöte* 78s',
'came home to Father choking on the floor'.

What do the waggons roll for, who will weigh
a Butlins in the pan with Buchenwald?
Death is a word in English. Gott is God.

And when I crawl from this cold absolute
of pointlessness I only step into
the meaner worries of the middle way.

Why are the ones I've loved so treacherous?
Where's the escape from unoriginality?
What courage could command a quiet end?

'I am myself indifferent honest but
yet I could accuse me of such things . . .'
Ophelias feel the heat of our self-hate.

And so fate faces both ways. My close loves
are matches for myself: can they forgive
my seeing my mediocrity in them?

DESKTOP CONFESSION

It is the brain which publishes our lives.
The fingers fight on any keyboard to
Invent the self, the total which survives,
The secret fundamentalist who
      Loves me but hasn't heard of you.

The screen lights up, the processor reveals
Its hoard of words, its everything that is;
The little brain is shocked, so it appeals
To death and summary, and 'Hers' and 'His'
      Are timed and ticked, with *sic* and *viz.*

Consider the girl whose head's between her legs,
Think of the minutes stalled in days and hours,
Making novels fly, grading rhymes like eggs—
The evanescent words, the paper flowers,
      The shifting Freudian lakes and towers,

These are confession's public instruments,
The only way a private voice can win.
Great houses send their several compliments,
This time you really get beneath the skin,
      You lift the lid and peer within.

Alas, there's nothing there to see; we come
From an unprinted blackness, one by one
Into the light; our books applaud and some
Live in our minds longer than things we've done,
      Old desktops warping in the sun.

BEDRIDDEN

There in a space like Lear's fired upland
We see them, the beds we've dreamed our lives in—
High, iron-framed, they wrap you like a mummy
In the cloths of dying, the toenailed sheets,
The blankets of the memory's understain—
Stored beneath them suitcases of letters,
Wine in cartons, tissues loved by moths,
Books fallen out of hands on to the dust.

These are the mirrored portages of life,
The tracks we took and once more didn't follow:
On their calm and terraced tracings
The sleeping mind has played the Emperor
To Everyman—a sort of slavery
Is all an ordinary terror can expect
Remote from the magniloquence of dreams,
A breakfast mind still sniping at its mail.

Such were the great ships of planning which
The Pharaohs built to sail in after death,
Made from what limits even gods on earth
To a belated laugh, and this is what
Your parents did for you, conceiving you
Upon a frame of casual fortune where
You'd lie in turn and make the world look down
To turn the pages of a picture book.

Now, like abandoned churches, beds adorn
The acreage of memory, lecturing
On treachery, quoting apocalypse,
Pure archaeology of randomness—
Here we hand on to others treasurable
Satisfactions of the race, a son's
Invisibility to God, a daughter's
Sacrament of beauty solemnized.

Danger is seen too late, the cry unmasked
As waking from a half-familiar storm
Devised by faces always swearing love
You feel the sides of where you lie, a real
If coffin-shaped, twice-reassuring place,
And start the channel where your parents passed
And feel the flow of paraphrase and reach
A wordless haven words might shelter in.

THE CHEQUE IS IN THE POST

Strange you can live so many years and now
discover a major condition of engagement—
namely that living is finding and tidying
love, this heap of whatever you were born with.

The house, the flat, the walls, the brooding books
relabel an old silence, the cowering quiet
emotion emotes against. The carpets and the bed,
things which react, call it contingency.

All agree on dreams. Those solid pieces break into
the flimsiness of day. They look askance
at circumstance's smudged vocabulary,
they can't get used to thinking's soft attack.

But the daydream chunters on in fitness
and misdeeds. It quickens by unfairness,
that and its outrage and the sheer *élan*
of indignation. Oh bliss to be betrayed!

Why will a funny God sit down with what
he's made and name it soul? He has in mind
a mind and knows that though each sports a leg
man and mosquito won't agree on pain.

To make the house a trained conventicle
the nomads must endure vanity,
lust's terse accommodation after doubt,
the smoother love which tilts a watering-can.

And face a constant shifting to the now.
Their words have dried them, they will blow across
the tundra or the campaign board until
demographers address them as the lost.

The cheque is in the post; the magistrate
glares at the shorthand writers, his aside
recorded, 'poisoned by philosophy',
as metaphor is called and takes the stand.

COAL SMOKE

He filters to the back of throat, a young man
    rigid with uncertainty,
breathing coal smoke from the evening air.

The writer in his sixties welcomes this
    returnee from eventfulness
and shows him to the body which is theirs.

The little cake dissolves, a sulphur taste
    deliquesces on the tongue—
evidence that the world exists for love.

1952 in London: fog closes in.
    The young man, older than his ghost,
looks to be delivered from himself.

1990, Lothian: the old man
    prepares to kill the forty years
he's fattened for his pungent prodigal.

THE VILLAGE EXPLAINER

The art of life is to be provincial;
to have sat in a plywood studio
for one's audition at the Quiz Kids'
Saturday Morning Jury,
to leave the shopping at the tram stop
but get home safely with the Cyclopaedia
of Submarines; to miss the waves of finches
in the wattle's volary because you wouldn't
lift your eyes from Audubon.

This way the fiction of assertion starts
and all the trumpets of controversy.
See the baby in his cot lift two fingers
in rebuke or benediction — dare his mother tell him
he's not the Pope? The blessing started
with the Fall, a myth to leer at
in the canvas seats of matinées, shared with
stencils of delight and death. Your ministry?
Café pulpits, those long hours at dawn
when the confessional cup is passed
and Mahler on the gramophone
abrades the torn wistaria — to travel,
to win disciples and to be depressed.

And so to the Enlightenment.
There will hardly be a Panel or a Column
you can't grace, or Round Table where Reality
is more than the rotating Chairman.
The March Past of the Words is now
a daily trooping, Understanding
plays its miniature overture, and
Self-Effacement looks into the glass.

Time makes even the autocue a blur
and this not uncourageous certainty
slides on to after-dinner mumbling,
the room emptying to your anecdotes —
back to the comforting provincialism
of dying, and if brave enough your joy
at finding out what can't be known.
Lastly, a reasonably long obituary

in the paper where you got your start,
The Village Explainer, in which old friends
remember how you milked the words the tribe
entrusted to you and the way you held
them spellbound, putting to them what they were.

BAD DREAMS IN VENICE

Again I found you in my sleep
And you were sturdily intact,
The counsel you would always keep
Became my dream's accusing tract.

Still I dared not think your force
Might even slightly slack my guilt —
This wasn't judgement but a course
Which self not knowing itself built.

It scarcely mattered where I dreamed,
The dead can choose a rendezvous:
You knew that nothing is redeemed
By blame, yet let me conjure you.

And this was Venice where we'd walked
Full tourist fig, first man and wife
On earth, and where we'd looked and talked
Your presence could outlive your life.

But now Venetian vapours clung
To every cold and wounding word —
The spectres which we moved among
Came from the phrases I had stirred.

They could not harm you but they bit
Into whatever had not died;
However we might reason it,
Your face and mine marched side by side.

And those old harshnesses which you
Muttered to me unrestrained,
Like Venice, loved but hated too,
Were all the closeness which remained.

BAD DREAMS IN NAPLES

My mind, that privatized Maecenas,
Has struck a bargain with my penis:
I dream a violent cityscape,
My feet stuck on with sellotape.

The boys of Spacca–Napoli
Are on their bikes pursuing me,
With girlfriends perched on hot machines,
Their labia outlined by their jeans.

I'm drinking Ischian white wine,
It's someone's piss, not even mine,
And now instead of riding pillion
My head is under Hugo Williams.

Around me genitals and faces
Appear in unexpected places—
A tap I chance to stand beside
Unzips my fly and feels inside.

I know what hurts me terribly,
The jokes and lack of dignity—
That fear should show contempt as well
Indubitably smacks of hell.

Yet this is better than the tilt
Which moves the action on to guilt.
A terrified and dying man
Is seeking his estranged wife's hand.

The Manager croons, con amore,
'No credit cards, please, Professore.'
I say my poetry will pay,
He shrugs and looks the other way.

They're packing me into my shroud.
I recognize it as the cloud
Always above Vesuvius.
My soul hangs round for God to suss.

So much for transcendentalism!
All the colours of the prism
When blended make one living light.
He breaks them up to keep them bright.

WISH WE WERE THERE

It would be our garden of scents and Spitfires,
it would be our yard for exercise,
it would go on for ever (and ever),
it would, of course, be Paradise.

And be fitted like a German kitchen,
every pleasantness at eye-level,
the cats on their curly yellow cat-mat
unequivocally of the Devil.

Mother and Father in frayed straw hats
and swatches of angelic flannelette,
the nimbus of childhood spreading wider,
the milkman trying to place a bet.

Getting old would be growing younger
as the CDs turn at 78
and Haydn's No. 97
provides a coda for Beethoven's Eighth.

The pet dogs buried by the roses
should rise from the limed and clayey soil
and the Council steamroller-driver
bring belated tears to the boil.

The post come twice a day from Youville
with letters of triumphant love —
you and Joseph on the river,
you with Fyodor by the stove.

And there too Indestructible Man
would keep death lurking by each bush,
clipping and pruning tirelessly,
the old lawnmower hard to push.

The voice of friendship calling up,
can you come down today to play
so time shall not move round the dial
and after-breakfast last all day.

The macaronic airs refresh us,
taking pity on a poor linguist
till it's Pentecost and Schubert's Miller
takes his withered flowers for grist.

The end is nigh but will not happen
as tea appears on the lawn—
the synchronicity of Heaven
is owed to us for being born.

VERB SAP

Nothing they say of this
Infinite mystery
    Love could disparage
More than its usual
Course through extremity
    Safe into marriage

High expectation of
Personal happiness,
    Magic achievement—
One takes on dozens of
Lovers, another stays
    High on bereavement—

Each plays the cold self game,
Seeing in love's face a
    Secret opponent
Where the advantage is,
Mirrored attraction or
    Pious atonement.

Poetry knows its role,
Lending its rhythms to
    All that's enduring,
Servitude, blandishment,
Irrationality,
    Even procuring.

STILL LIFE WITH CATS

Once more I thank you beasts: you have delivered me
from the scrutiny of time's inspectorate
nor have you insisted on alternative philosophies,
endurance, love of limits or the world in little —
you know expectedness and a sort of
charity keep meals arriving and a few good rubs
attract a stroking if the biped god is kind:
the rest's captivity, the freely starving birds
mocking you at third-floor window sills,
the tray behind the door a sponsored graveyard
where dreams of freedom waft the death-smell out,
but you are moving firmly through our rooms
defining objects, a whole cosmology of glass
and cushions, stipulating with a yawn and outstretched paw
the anti-matter of the visible. Supremacists
of what is there, cats are the Chardins and Latours
of inner-city living.
                        This room has lost its focus,
no cat is in it. I am left with vanity
of pens and speakers, panel-lights, chrysanthemums
drooping now to dusk. Our human scale is sadness
giving readings of selective understanding
and when some happiness obtrudes it weighs like ornate bowls
bearing the fruits and flowers of imagining.
                        Then the cats will say, trotting through
a suddenly opened door, 'you had forgotten us
and our sharp needs, painting your pretty picture,
unnatural living is still life, you know . . .'
                        and I will lead them back
into the kitchen where the sacred loaves
and fishes wait in tins and boxes, and the light
switched on makes sermons of necessity.

AWAKENING OF PLEASANT FEELINGS
UPON ARRIVING IN THE COUNTRY

I was talking to a tree near Kettering,
admitted straight away
I didn't know its sort—a kind of
beech or hornbeam, rather spindly,
not well placed beside a fallen gate,
too close to the railway and scuffed
by cows and sheep—
       Nearby and all around
more nearly noble oaks and sycamores
and even the odd cedar rubbed the sky,
with semi-undismantled hedgerows,
willows scraping the canal
and gardens dragging through
the lees of autumn—
       I could barely envision
a less romantic landscape,
one made more derelict by men's
necessary sad encouragements—
       Imagine my surprise
when with a dark percussion of its leaves
it answered me—
       'Vain as your fears
of dying, the contusion of the planet
in a frame of fire, is your love
of Nature, the tall Wordsworthian glare
which turns green fields to templates,
douses in a swill of Technicolor
the rooted struggle of articulation.
       We have no Pantheon,
just a clinging to the soul of water,
a light-filled ruthlessness which hoists
a canopy on every hurt.
       Argue with the earth
and lose your way: the only life which counts
is any system which won't shift its ground.
Set in the soil, it lives and dies
where it was made. Life was a jousting
of two modules once: it's now a raggedness
of old survivors looking at the sky,
ungraded, blank, beyond nomenclature.'

PIGEONS, GULLS AND STARLINGS

Imagine a heaven where every one of these
is known by bar codes on its wings or tail.

Where someone cares beyond importing them
into an apophthegm about survival.

Better for them to stick to their concourse
of things abutting, edges without flighting.

We like to think they clean the wounds of feeling,
the scabs which form around dependency.

It's not that they like scorpions will survive
the fire storm, just that they aren't concerned.

A philosopher might teach one how to talk
and find it walked right past philosophy.

Yet a bird could share with a philosopher
the poverty of dreaming one dream always.

The syncopation of our kindness: we
shoo them from the lawn when wood-doves land.

They can't be rare and lovable, or mime
their gratitude like hungry ducks ashore.

Come *The Last Supper* in the Park, they know
France's premier chef is named L'oiseau.

They've been with Jesus and at Venice, viz.
renowned St Gull's, St Pigeon's and St Stare's.

Pray for the sadness of intelligence,
the many lives envisaged in the one.

FAINTING GOATS

So then, on the road,
what you took for a blue-flanked bus
smothered you in dust,
not a Pauline plunge
just agnostic reflexes
pricking against the kicks.

In San Pantalon
looked upwards at a mess of angels,
forgot to make the art-historical dismissal,
had to sit down hurriedly—
'gobsmacked in God's Supermarket',
'as tasteless as eternity',
'the wrong side of the Grand Canal'.

Guessed from this
that words are not housetrained,
told the dream you were sorry
but you had another engagement.

Looked on appalled
as love, called to the telephone,
collapsed on the carpet
still clutching the receiver—
was it the Heavy Breather
or only his answering machine?

Conceived of a mountain pass—
suddenly round the corner
loomed a stranger on the path—
Max Miller perhaps,
the Button Moulder,
Moses with the tablets?

In a vision
touched their soft coats,
gazed in their angora eyes,
these plaintive fainters who know
how much there is
to be afraid of in the world.

There were shepherds abiding in the fields,
came then the tramontana—

Atishoo, atishoo,
we all fall down.

IN ROSEWELL

These small, well-built and greystone Lothian houses
Seem full of sadness, ringed about by sky.
Unlike the flock of birds my presence rouses
Their dignity will wait till I go by.
Perhaps they feel that one who lives in books
Is hardly worth a turbulence of rooks.

The birds have high trees and a castled river
To underwrite their screaming senate's noise
As down the wet roads juggernauts deliver
Animals to death, and cycling boys
Pass kennels where impounded dogs and cats
Howl to the lonely lawns and council flats.

How should a writer better test self-pity
Than standing soaked outside the Miners' Club
With letters of importance for some city
And far too shy to go into the pub?
I bring my quiet burden to the post,
A lifetime's correspondence with a ghost.

WOKEN AT NOON

Good little liberals, the crocuses
    Are leading discussion groups on Spring,
      The best of focuses
        Is lengthening.

Roses of fear, trimmed by a loving father,
    Ours are the tight blooms up the drive,
      Not honey, pollen rather
        From a dark hive.

Miracles are never kind, they thrust
    Us back on our distinctive ends;
      Angels pass, we trust
        The talk of friends.

Childhood found a way with facts, collected
    Them like postage stamps and then
      Picked the resurrected
        Parts up again.

We judge by touching, always raising pitch,
    An analogue of love and lover;
      The metaphor is rich
        But gives no cover.

Market forces rule across all levels —
    In hell, most orthodox of places,
      You learn to know the devils
        By their faces.

OVERHEARD AND UNDERPHRASED

It was Happy Hour
at the Café Helicon.
Ever since boredom
made the ratings
a good crowd had
beetled in to hear
the big ones talking
or just to look
at the ever-changing
faces at top table.
What was the conversation like?
people wanted to know.
It's not a pick-up,
it's an eavesdrop place,
Olympian mirror-alley,
they knew that. One
asked a waiter. Well, he said,
they'd been rabbiting on
about the new faces
in the Sundays, not the slags
and gossip-writers, but
the communicators, bards
and moralists.
They didn't like it. It cut
across their territory.
But they could wear it.
After all, said Zeus,
just take Sappho
and Cassandra, what
does it come to, their stuff,
surely it's just that people like
hearing girls talk dirt?

ANATOMY LESSON

So long since passing through the epidermis
We may forget the outer casements of
This curious pale: we are in an echo-theatre
Where the central dynamo continues purring
In inviolate light. Here are the power points,
Their names and functions, the famished trades
Which must prevail. So much has been revealed
And yet we cannot sight the seed of terror
Planted here. Watered in dreams, it grows
To harvest size in pure hallucination
And hangs another world behind the eyes.
Then the great factory reappears—a wreck
With ribs deep in sand, a woman's body
Booby-trapped, pleasure gardens fringed
By poisoned plants. The words in latin on
The labels are disguises for our ignorance,
The hired cassettes purr culture-speak—'just one
Consequence of an evolutionary leg-up',
'Without this fear we never would have
Outsoared the plants and animals' . . . they send us
To the distant tower where words are made,
Where data are transformed by tribal wish.
Destroy this living library, it won't
Be Alexandria burning to the water,
Merely a setback to an integer.
Finally the knowledge is absorbed
In all description and all mystery,
The code of copulation and amplexus.
We close the body up and move to more
Conjectural cavities: we seek at last
The nervous gardens and the plains of Hell,
The parenthetic walls of Paradise.

THE IRRADIATED POEM

It has been exposed to safe bombardment
Of formalistic and idealist rays,
Hölderlin's mad Hellenism and Dante's
Tuscan spite; Grand Masters of the Usual
Have lent their dailiness to what it says;
It will not stale through evenings of
Impossibilist ethics; nor will Modernism's
Janus gaze unsettle its decorum,
Reading backwards to a heritage
Or forward into unsupported shapes
Of art. The world is learning on its way
To entropy: we can keep our poems fresh
With digital robotics, dots for deeds.
The secret is in essences—consider
A strobe of Wordsworth on his lake patrol:
To separate the wonder and the fervour
From his paper stamps and stale rememberings,
The cottage diction and the drying nappies,
This will show now on the modern screen,
A self-insuring shadow, lettered love.
Untouched by human mind, this packaged work
Is yet encoded with those proving slights
Which sound technique has raised above the mire—
Haven't poems always snuggled down
In stout anthologies the better to forget
The wrecks of hate they were constructed from?
These things are now themselves but troped
In sunshine and in cleanliness,
All made in factories of insightfulness
And marketed responsibly. The rare,
The suicidal, calamitously dreamt,
Become pure style, an ogling of the dark,
An epic for our breakfast rooms compatible
With toast and radio. The Odyssey
Is on a jug and someone is collecting
Rebel Angels, the whole series, out of packets
Lanced by winter light. A Golden Age
Which cares for poems dawns once more and they,
Delighted to be useful, give interviews
To busy journalists. Who says the world
Can not unlock its brutal doors or that

The Muses will not wear white coats? The Inward
Shines through outwardness and we no longer need
A sickness in our words to make us write.

This poem is certified safe to read.

APOTHEOSIS OF THE SHORT POEM

It has to run to thirteen lines to kit
the Devil out and yet avoid the sonnet;
death should be reflected in its hub-caps
but never named; rhyming, scanning and devices
of ludic and linguistic stitching-up
can be to taste, and so a field
of lightly-planted language poetry
might suffice; Blake and The Palatine
Anthology, Altenberg and Landor,
Mabel Lucie Attwell, Emily upstairs —
the enormous Self attains apotheosis
in a bonsai belvedere, its elder eye
misting over as Susanna bathes.

THE CHAIR OF BABEL

We are in the fashionable Republic of Evil
for an especially relevant conference.

My neighbour has been first on his feet
after each paper with a question.

I see from his conference entry
he has the Chair of Babel
in a taxidermist's country.

Unfortunately it's so hot
we keep the windows open and the noise
of traffic fillets every sentence.

Half of us speaks one language and half
another, though their half knows ours well
and our half's monoglot.

The official translator is a genius—
'The lady says her case is near-Hegelian'
he likes to start—

This morning my neighbour asked
'Why do Schubert's lieder hymn the sea
and fisher-folk when he had seen no stretch
of water wider than a lake?'

The translation went: 'The landlocked mind
will ever seek an amniotic . . .'

I turned my headphones on and heard
'The camera runs, the wildcat eats the hare . . .'

The noise at coffee-break is settling down
at about G below middle C, I guess.

At lunch yesterday two conferenciers
had their bags stolen by youths who rode
mopeds through the restaurant.

Case histories tend to leap from
shit and bonding to repair
ignoring counter-transference.

We are united in distrusting one old man
whose sense of humour is exaggerated.

Viz., he said, 'This reminds me of
Judge Schreber's childhood harness which only .
Houdini could have masturbated in.'

I've seen one car which halted at the lights
but that was when they'd turned to green.

A Venezuelan hung around with gold
suggested we imagine suicide
as a function of God's Repo-Firm.

The conference is in a palace
with *trompe l'oeil* walls
seemingly adjacent to Arcadia.

I dream of people making love inside my body
quite unconcerned that I am watching them.

But now I know what we are here for—
it's in the Bible, that club of confidences—

A buzz of international cooperation
doubtless held hubristic somewhere else.

Stuffed melanzane and fizzy wine
are served beside old fish ponds
by the light of floating tapers.

I say to my neighbour,
daring to speak to him at last,
'Is yours a big department?'

'We have Gossip, Pentecost,
Green Vocabulary,
Eye Utterance
and Cultspeak,' he replies.

The plane to take us home
is blessed by several Cardinals
and provided by
The Cooperative Society of Ghosts.

WITTGENSTEIN'S DREAM

I had taken my boat out on the fjord,
I get so dreadfully morose at five,
I went in and put Nature on my hatstand
And considered the Sinking of the Eveninglands
And laughed at what translation may contrive
And worked at mathematics and was bored.

There was fire above, the sun in its descent,
There were letters there whose words seemed scarcely cooked,
There was speech and decency and utter terror,
In twice four hundred pages just one error
In everything I ever wrote—I looked
In meaning for whatever wasn't meant.

Some amateur was killing Schubert dead,
Some of the pains the English force on me,
Somewhere with cow-bells Austria exists,
But then I saw the gods pin up their lists
But was not on them—we live stupidly
But are redeemed by what cannot be said.

Perhaps a language has been made which works,
Perhaps it's tension in the cinema,
Perhaps 'perhaps' is an inventive word,
A sort of self-intending thing, a bird,
A problem for an architect, a star,
A plan to save Vienna from the Turks.

After dinner I read myself to sleep,
After which I dreamt the Eastern Front
After an exchange of howitzers,
The Angel of Death was taking what was hers,
The finger missed me but the guns still grunt
The syntax of the real, the rules they keep.

And then I woke in my own corner bed
And turned away and cried into the wall
And cursed the world which Mozart had to leave.
I heard a voice which told me not to grieve,
I heard myself. 'Tell them', I said to all,
'I've had a wonderful life. I'm dead.'

HIS BODY TO BLAISE PASCAL

Dear Monitor, I have lived too long
with discipline, I have become a boil
of parable; I can hardly stop myself
making pus from meditation.
        I am vain of green,
of salad gardens; roses my carbuncles,
water for carnations my recourse
to free blocked tears; nature seen in windows
not on pen-stands. You have promulgated
No other religion has proposed that we
should hate ourselves. No other religion then
can please whoever hates himself. Steam
unfolds in wrappings of the sick-bed, pain
tastes like lightning, and in storms I see
your torn connectives building Heaven until
the world is one ridiculous proposal.
        Truth's a freelance god
and mathematics is his muse. I have
been converted like a Janissary and
compelled to serve the lord of immolation;
you have made me one of dying's mercenaries
ranging through the morning's hapless streets.
        To exclude reason,
to admit no other thing but reason: your arrows
miss the butt—to have the flush of sickness
by equation, politicos of splendour
built on dreams, and think it all from Moses
not the body's storehouse!—O stars
far off, spread light on me; you only glow
inside a mad humility.
        We are being trained
to live our very living without life—
instead of narrowing through glass the sun
on pigeons' wings, a shaman-spirit toils
by candlelight at revelation, yeasts
of fear to make deception physical.

Cromwell was about
to ravage Christendom but a little
grain of sand got into his bladder. You know,
my host, we cannot bank on grains of sand
incising us on God's memorials.
                    you gained me as a mule,
today you walk me like a hospital;
I am your body and would be your friend
but can't act as confessional: my grille
shows nothing of a face and ears beyond,
no listener with untainted breath. Job sat
in chiaroscuro while the world recoiled
to salt, his cities axioms of comfort—
are Hebrew letters your false comforters?
                    Incomprehensible
that the world should be created
and incomprehensible that it should not.
The starlit stairs, the movement of a viol string,
an adding-machine's projection of the soul—
whichever mystery you choose will prove
you wrong. To doubt the animal in me
will not goad God. That's death, an ordinary
fellow difficult to dislike—he knows
that you and I pay taxes here. He's coming
with abrupt continuo to liberate
the one and many from innumeracy.

TRICKY LITTLE MAGDALENE

The membrane separating this world
from its other is wafer-thin
and only sex sustains it.

The Last Post and the Lost Past sound together,
childhood through the rain-swept queues
shows dogs fucking at your trouser-cuffs
and Uncle Mick leaving Circular Quay
with Resch's Dinner Ale and a bottle of oysters
wrapped in the evening paper.

After the light shows and the Edwardian whiskers
a gift for drawing—grandeur and decline
are chiaroscuro,
the knights ride on the ice
and here a drunken woman falls to the ground
masturbating through her skirt
outside our chic Belphoori.

This androgyne Belshazzar
giggles as a hefty Rapunzel
curtains his genitals with her hair.
What's going on behind? Certainly
he's got his toes in her ravine:
it helps the ecstasy to find sex funny,
then you can put these things where they need to go,
in the hole created for our trickiness.

No, we are not doing the dirt on sex
or finding it repulsive
but considering Freud's pet vulture
as she parts our lips with her tail feathers
and brings us to the world's workface.

Is this the Obscurity Principle,
the laziness of imagination,
a doing-without-significance,
or is it instead the Obscenity Principle
where all the happy tales of hobbits
and witches inside mirrors
are pornography for men afraid of women?

The sex-chain is a food-chain.
Eat your mother till you are her,
steal from Daddy's well-stocked plate
and go down greedily on Goldilocks.
The chants of cannibalism
float down from a cantoria
so quattrocentro, such a frieze
of angels proudly edible,
The Last Supper everlastingly laid out.

Of course, the best course is Repentance
for which you need a feast of sin.
God's little joke is in two worlds
and coming from the other
we have no memory of it
and going thither again
we will not know what we have been
once back in that occluded air. The scene's
a football crowd, an orgy, a party
at the zoo—the caption reads
'They shall not die', and Magdalene
stands up for Jesus, your parents open
the picture books of history,
the cruiser Aurora fires her salvoes,
jacaranda smoulders on the garden path
as Granny Main, stiff in her lacy black,
lifts her veil and shows you down the steps
to the dark places of inheritance.

A TOUR OF THE CITY

In the tenth week of the siege
I discovered I could triplicate my limbs
and looked bemusedly at my six arms
lying parallel in the bath.

The enemy had built a tower
which out-topped our walls and thus they must soon
move against us. Sieges, of course,
had long since ceased to happen
but fear of dying musked the air,
a seriousness glossed by caricature.

Suddenly I could not bear to look,
the gods were walking by our gates,
star-poultices against their eyes
to stem the glare of our carnality.

The body can't hold ecstasy:
I clasped them to me
knowing they were exactly what they seemed,
the huge and radiant intercessors
whom books and nerves have sanctified
in every generation—and the joy
of talking with them raised the siege,
I could tell my friends we were beloved,
these ancient specialists would contrive
an exile for us, not a final death.

The timed naturalness of their skin,
enjambment of intensity and fate,
could co-exist with tractable delight—
their conversation was of Irish priests
who baptised long cigars, their choruses
a clawback from Euripides
and chocolate nightingales.
I cried for sheer simplicity
as though I took an everlasting heart
from my long-buried mother. The siege was time
and would be brought again but they would know
a passage through the vines, a blood funicular.

They had the dryness of encyclopaedias,
a wide disclaimer like a page which opens
on a saffron lake with fish-nets drying
and a castle lapped by water; their halcyon
was the opposite of miracles,
the first hours of a holiday, your mouth
finding its own way to hot bagels,
ahead a terrace lunch, a via dolorosa
lined with moulting figs. The blurred gods
were the first tourists and true pathfinders —
it is hilarious to meet them, Lady Hesters
under veils of lightning, translating
the epodes of a Montenegrin shepherd.

The whole world was their city and they took
my hand and led me to the parapet
and showed me which great doors were closed,
what cupboards Bluebeard kept the keys of
and which departing buses knew the road.
In my bath two arms now seemed enough,
the skylight garlanded the sun — outside
the city simmered and the gods were gone,
back to the paper of their ecstasy.

THE CARTRAC QUATRAINS

The deaf man at the ranting rail
Thought Ulysses by the mast a liar
To dare the supernatural lewd
Yet give it flesh in which to dwell.

They'd travelled troubled miles through maps
On nothing more than hope and spam.
From figurehead to galley rats
The whole crew sought a landward star.

The Chief would tell their chancy saga
To any girl, call it a gas—
King's daughter, sorceress or diva,
His salty words made each one avid.

They'd passed beyond the sucking pool,
The chute of soot, the strangling loop,
They'd trembled at the giant's step
And put baits out for Circe's pets.

Up at the helm, an unmoved slob
Swilled his mouth with heavy Bols
And from the sleep of tainted pork
Devils came, a spectral crop.

Philosophers had taught them time
Is infinite, that skies emit
Ill luck alone and in the trap
Of hope endurance plays its part.

And now they sulked in Venus' cart
Along some star-directed track,
The sea their home, a final coma
Where death and memory run amok.

FLAGS OF CONVENIENCE

His trouble was he was too easily awed
Yet when absurdity and fear were wed
His speech of warm congratulation made
Implicit reference to a world gone mad.

Then twice he was the hero with the wound,
The Magic Bowman, The Keeper of Christ's Tear,
Discovering as bandages unwound
That where the soul would speak the flesh must tear.

And looked within a vile and feasting pie
For childhood faces; set sail from the pier
When dawn winds fought the harbour undertow;
Hid as the decoy trundled through the town.

Asked of the tongues of aunties on his couch
Above ancestral streets if this might lead
By creeping groundsel and suburban couch
To coffined scarlet or laconic lead.

The language knew its duty, what to know
And how to make him say it, so that now
He found his words insisting what he said
Be packed in stanzas, ready like First Aid.

NEIGHBOURS

I am Ceccho de Cecchi
who died in 1493
and I apologize now
for troubling you.
This is my chance to speak,
all because a book
is open at my entry—
that's my name, a key
record for the month, but nobody's
heard of me I've been dead
so long. I was important, I led
a useful life and was a devout
Christian, true husband and
a businessman of good repute.
You who read my name,
quite a few of you will be nobodies
compared to me—please
understand how I long
in this dark to be back among
my fellows and my reputation,
how lonely it is here
where we are forgotten. Days, I know,
must lengthen into shadow,
but let me talk to you.
I remember we'd sing Mass
and beyond our voices we would hear
the cries of pigs being slaughtered
for the coming feast. We listened
to our own ends but we felt
only the excellent wind
of fortune which fans the young.
Now time has torn out my tongue.
On the opposite page, level with me,
is another faded entry—
for October 1492—
in the Libro dei Morti
of Borgo San Sepolcro—
'died on the twelfth, Piero
di Benedetto di Francesco,
painter'. Pray for me
and for all immortality.

A PSALM BEFORE THE SAUSAGES

Enter now the irresponsibility of ants
whose workload is sheer slavery but whose
hearts are hardened by inconsequence.

The little plums are rotting on the tree
uncultivated: a beautiful holiday sky
hangs over a land which smells of shit.

Every part from hoof to anus goes
into these calm torpedoes on the grill.
Their benediction spatters on your glasses.

And the lost alluvial finch sings on the roof
above the prowling cat. You could believe
some mighty hand made these arpeggios.

The constructed and the natural conspire together:
trucks head into Vence and at Coursegoules
clouds arrange a meeting-point at sea.

Transfiguration seems just rearrangement,
the foot in sandals near the naked breast,
equivalences without synonyms.

High above the baou a spotter plane
circles for fires, the country's soul on show—
they drag Madonna through the air at Nice.

The labouring woodlouse needs a miracle
to live another day, and we have plans
which reach into the next millennium.

'Slink-tink', 'slink-tink', cicadas start: the sun
undoes the knotted brain and the great harp
of sausages plays to its only Lord.

THE RIVAL POET

His work shines through the spaces of your thought
So crystalline for being words in stars
And phrased as if our blood itself could speak.

The world he sees is cuneiform for God
But he is free of moral adjuncts, dining
With names and beauties in allusive dachas.

He has the dangerous beard of a Tuscan
Innovator early dead: you see
Him strut like Tolstoy on his own estate,

Each peasant pregnant by him; he has flowers
At his fingertips which praise the land
While you are keyboard-bound and colourless.

Call him a louche Longinus and he'll smile
And dangle a child upon his knee and scan
The family snapshots for sublimity.

The first to make a picture picture its
True self in diagram, he lets his mind
Recapture infantile omnipotence.

His pre-shrunk paradise is metaphor,
A crossword puzzle running out of clues
Till even death-beds start to stink of skill.

It is your vanity to be his Other,
Erecting trellises of words to keep
The world suspended in the winds of time.

Two politicians of the printed page,
You both are talking to a vacant moon.
The tongueless stones have said it all before.

LISTENING TO SHAKESPEARE

I was at school with him
that Will Shakespeare,
carved his name on his desk,
pissed on it to make it shine,
edited a magazine called *Nova*
the name of our river spelled backwards—
he said we should always remember
that words were the way you told lies
and got out of a walloping—
he got us to compare our penises
and said one boy's was Small Latin
and another one's Less Greek,
he kept us entertained with faces
and wrote endless essays
when he wasn't courting.

When he went to London
I was really sorry. Or was it Lancashire?
Anyway we heard of him in London,
then his Dad got into trouble about church
and his Old Woman sulked at home
and we had several discontented winters.
One day I met him in the High Street,
he seemed a bit furtive,
said the chap loitering on the corner
was a government spy,
'haven't I got trouble enough with Coriolanus?'
I loved his stories from the classics
but it only made him gloomy,
'You know what Marston told me,
all Penelope did in Ulysses' absence
was fill Ithaca full of moths—
why come back when the moths at home
are never going to change to butterflies?'
I showed him a review in the local paper,
'Stratford author's sour-note sonnets'.
He wasn't interested and talked
about the price of real estate.

But he was big in London,
you heard about it even here.
And all the time he bought up property
and made himself a gentleman
like his father had tried but failed to do.
Then he came home, old and tired,
saying if life's race were run from eleven to ninety
he was at the ninety end
though all of forty-eight.
Once at an Open Day he said mysteriously
'Congratulations, you have just invented
a new art form—let's call it Local History
and hurry it along to Heritage.'

We listened when he talked to us.
I used to love his high harangueing
but it died away. He died too,
quite suddenly. Managed a good tomb
before the altar and no digging-up
and stowing in the ossuary. I've kept a note
he passed me under the desk once
during a long grammar lesson.
'No man may know a neighbour closer
than his own defeat. The unfolding star
calls up the shepherd. Soon there'll be
nothing of the world to listen to.'

IN ECCLESIA

For the Honour of Italy

Oh how they feared my caterpillar rages,
I sang in flesh as robins roar in cages.
Siena the well-pleached would slumber on,
The truant Pope skulk still in Avignon.

I brought him home, I wrote a thousand letters,
I prayed with axemen and harangued my betters.
To starve the faith the Commune practised caution,
No loaves, no fishes, just the sinner's portion.

God's secretary once, now Italy's,
How can I pray, I cannot bend my knees?
In Santa Maria Sopra Minerva, boned,
In San Domenico, a skull enthroned.

2

A Field-Day for the Baroque

Chill water everywhere brought by the Popes
And high tech ruins clinging to the slopes —
Whichever Rome you like is on the clock,
The hands, alas, keep pointing at Baroque.

From Sant' Andrea al Quirinale
To twisted baldacchinos of God's barley-
sugar, Baroque has loosed its loyal genie —
A Berni Inn compared with Borromini.

Now try St Ivo alla Sapienza,
The dome's a calibrated light condenser.
Geometry has lanced the site for pus
To spurt on God, but shower gold on us.

SACRA CONVERSAZIONE

We're here to help old Dosso out,
there's gentle Joseph, John the Bap,
a saint the donor heard about
and Mary, me—and Him, of course,
the Babe I'm holding in my lap,
no room for angel, sword or horse.

We were alive once—that's to say
I think we're more than legendary
but what the picture has to say
despite how very real we look
is Keep your eye on Emily,
Make sure the keys are on the hook.

You'll have to ask this little Bugger,
the focus of our family pic,
doctor, lawyer, rugger-bugger
when He grows up, the point of it,
this lovely world which makes us sick—
we don't know how the hell we fit.

You doubt that folks like us could get
our picture painted by a top
professional (so hard to get)—
we hear you sniff behind our back,
art lovers scoffing escalope,
'This lot's the sort for a Big Mac.'

It's symbolism, can't you tell,
the low raised up, the high cast down,
as paints and words and notes foretell:
Heaven's a sort of Hollywood
and Dosso's hot on evening gowns—
who gives a shit who's great and good?

A TALE OF TWO PIETIES

One God, one Prophet now we celebrate:
Christ and Mohammed at the going rate.

The Christian God's six hundred years the elder,
He's almost learned He cannot be the State,

Though once as Christendom He spanned the world
And lit his fires to feed the great debate.

The modern liberal shudders as he reads
That martyrs hold all doubt degenerate.

Not just foul Popes but Milton, Donne and Blake
Said love despised returns again as hate.

The Christian world had wars—the Seven, the Thirty,
Hundred Years—with blood like streams in spate,

And if in our Home Counties now the faith
Is shrunk to prose and flower-arrangement—wait

Until our troops come home once more triumphant,
The God of Battles passes round the plate.

The younger faith has long been in eclipse
That once with scimitars flashed to the gate

Of Old Vienna. The Alhambra and Khayaam
Delight us more than Suleiman the Great,

Which makes it easy to forget the tics
Of singlemindedness which adumbrate

The once and only Truth of the Koran—
No other glorious word has any weight!

No chance of jokes, or satire, ambiguity,
No room for God like Mankind to migrate—

Just a murderous present, a great heat,
A wish for death, spontaneous and innate.

Redeemers always reach the world too late.
God dies, we live; God lives, we die. Our fate.

RULES TO THE EXCEPTION

The great good of the one is not a cause.
Effective power settles into laws.
The liturgy was made from broken rules.
The words of love become the names of schools.

To imitate the Saviour stay obscure.
The brightest object in a trap's the lure.
Theology, we're taught, makes better art.
How many angels surface in a fart.

Until the rules are written, no one wins.
The bits which fall on that side are called sins.
Most gods have tempers like their worshippers.
The cat that's tickled is the cat which purrs.

This church was built to house a piece of bone.
The stair to Heaven rises tone by tone.
Ecstatic truth includes the ludicrous.
What people die for must be serious.

Id, Ego, Super Ego, Trinity!
The Devil's bell calls hermits in to tea.
It happened long ago in picture books.
The brochure for Mt Athos is at Cooks.

Pascal took issue even with perfection.
You see the danger of divine election.
Great minds exhibit great credulity.
This fervent space of doubt is filled with Me.

The possible begins with a Big Bang.
The dawn of pain was what the angels sang.
The seventh day was set apart for rest.
The Blessed are hard to tell from the Depressed.

A CLUMSY CATECHISM

What is the purpose of our life?
Question the butter why the knife
Goes through it, clear the pond of weed
And watch rapscallion beetles breed.

What power put us on the earth?
The lack of rhyme, the pious dearth
Of consequence, the one-way flow
Of dripping curds through calico.

What is the challenge of the New?
A freshness of the morning dew
Turned automatic hosing-down
Of thoroughfares throughout the town.

What do we mean by tragedy?
A rather bigger you and me
Than any that our neighbours know—
Fire in Heaven but lights below.

What, after all this time, is truth?
Research reveals that Pilate's tooth
Was troubling him, he couldn't stay
Debating with the Bench all day.

Where may an honest man be found?
The singer hears a different sound
Inside his head than discs record,
Herbert alone can say, *My Lord*.

What is the reason for our death?
To find the only rhyme for breath,
To bottom-out both Blake and Dante,
The genius proved, the Profit scanty.

BRIDES COME TO THE POET'S WINDOW

Birds, it should have been, but pleasure quickens
As the white and peregrine performers land.

Such chattering of all the hopeful starts
Like trees renewing their hay-fever wraps;

Cool shadows, straight and ordinary,
To startle the recluse's whisky dreams.

Each bride is decked in her uncertainty,
Her jokes are uncles, sex a limousine

And in the ride to the abyss she hears
With doubtful face the radiant hymn swell up.

These are the frescoes of a fallen world,
The flocks of sulphur-crested cockatoos,

The parrots which don't read the City Pages,
Corporate worms indifferent to Darwin.

Where else, how otherwise devise a world
Where God is in his place and Heaven's a sight,

Where boredom does the artwork, misery
The economic planning and petulance

Sends the invitations? Our daughter's wedding
Was the day we decided to separate.

The poet in his cell is sneezing with
The pollen of the breeding world; he blows

His nose of sheets of multi-stanza'd white —
Is he obliged to fizz his own champagne?

O Brides of Solomon, did no one tell you
You're merely symbols of a loving God,

That high erotic temperatures are just
Visions of Paradise on fading silk?

In the painted garlands of the Farnesina
The melons, halved, glisten in future light.

YOU MIGHT HAVE RHYMED

But I was busy putting things in order,
like language so Shakespeare could write his plays,
and stamens and pistils for the bees
and waves to carry surfboards to the beach
ending up among the winking needles —
The details can be peculiar, viz.
something I saw on television, a tray
of skulls seeming like arteries in mutton
or gargoyle mouths from Gaudi's own stockpile —
These details have the numbers:
think of me as the biggest chip of all
and always in the present. In the poet's play
you get a video of important men
fighting over a backyard and its souls —
The immortal liveliness is mine,
I underwrite it with a fear of death,
a monstrous burden on my conscience, yes,
but you won't expect me to face everyone
who has a clause to plead to, nor amend
some workable few rules which can't be made
to square with justice. Originally this was
to be an experimental place, a sort
of trout farm I could leave apprentices
to run, but it got out of hand. The trouble
must be language — I know you think it's tears
and blood and all the mess that's left behind
at death, the swellings of incontinence —
But words are worst, the devil's advocates
(I can pinch a good phrase when I need to) —
they're ratchets on the running-on of time,
my most precise invention. Worse still
they're plausible simplicities that woo
the brain from complication. I stir the avant-garde
(my best fifth column) to put a shine
on this opacity but meaning still
pokes through — It's Vallombrosan leaves
and epigrams at sundown as the world
gets out the chairs for its crepuscular chit-chat
and puts it nerves on watch. And as I said
I made the stuff originally, the words I mean,
not just the sexual nucleii and space

so limitless it must engross itself.
I've watched the human creature come
into his inheritance and known he'd scatter
his poor bones among the charcoal glow
of Nature. I'm tired of perfection
almost made, of legends born in gardens
and words of faith exchanged at dusk
but just this once I'll listen to your prayer
and so amend my well-loved son's quatrain:
For thou dost know, O Damon dear
This realm dismantled was
Of Jove himself: and now reigns here
A very God because . . .

EXHALATIONS OF THE ABSTRACT

It's right to take the key of family terror
And so unlock the old bureau to find
Some estimables to offer to the market,
And the key will be inside a drawer stuffed
With dreams and hankies—the old key furred with fear
Fits every strong-box when the one tune plays
In manner as a friend epitomized
Beside the hospital TV, his cool
Enjambment of security and fright
Approving all the engineering words
Which publish Babel and defy concern—
Then with the proper slinking gait of one
Elected to portray Pandora watch them fly
To do their patent harm, the photos, packets,
Feathers from the Punjab, filed under
Stranded love and streaming out to kill.

Thus even the phlegmatic principles
Of true responsibility relax
To watch those starry whirrings up above
And trace through some black text book what this means
As inner fire: worlds of ice and dust
Appear on monitors and say they're real
Though mouthing electronics as they go
To amplify credulity, and this
Cohabits with the dugong's smile, the lights
On tuners and the panelled envelopes.
All language is of objects and the rose
Surprising you above the window sill
Is one strayed word returning to the fold,
A dividend exacted from abstraction.
Among the dead the aunts have not relaxed
Their stark vocabulary and prune for hope.

So, craving all the sharps and flats, the ear
Explores its puffy mathematics and
The ups and downs of rules which make the earth
A sheet of paper from a tired computer—
Give me a child at five and I will make
Him numerate with God, say fantasists of line
Whose blood can analyse to triangles—

Watch me sail like Bach across the moon,
My feet on pedals of the Saxon greed,
States one maturely, all his variations
Claimed in canon. Otherwise in gloom
A tiered inheritance must bring the gout
And grief of genealogies to
The present door and only hackers of
The screened sublime will taste the honey made
For us and stored in combs of inequality.

THE CAMP

Nobody believes it will be permanent
yet none is just a visitor—
those are the visitors, the horrified with low-calorie drinks
and flowers in candy-strata'd paper,
trying to identify their cards
among the book-and-fruit-strewn chests-of-drawers.

These inmates hate the outside world
but not their kapos
who if they are good will one day
put the all-forgiving pills in magic quantity
into their night-time milk.

Nurses excuse a sentinel complicity
with self-abstracted smiles.
If they were to break the high taboo of truth
their prisoners would know beyond a doubt
they had been wicked
and would recognize their punishment.
'Look-who-I've-brought-to-see-you'
is camp language for the cull to come
which may even be tonight.

Say six are in a room,
each his or her Sargasso moored around,
none will want to know who these five are
nor tell an outside spy one fact or name.
To pity noises in the night would be unthinkable—
the breakfast angel wheels a new day through
the straggling outer cantonments.

Now comes inspection by the Commandant
who may prefer preferment
in the open air to these exiguous duties—
he has a nod for each inveterate
and an eye for change
as finely calibrated as a rain gauge.

Yet there are annunciations.
Perhaps one plaintive afternoon
touching on the sibylline
hope's cruel consistency
condescending out of memory
will conjure eyes past cloudy windows
to a place where luck can happen
and show between the bed and shadow
something leaning over whispering love.

There has been a brief rebellion.
A veteran spoke of terror, screamed resentfully
at the pastel walls—now all is quiet
and experiment is started once again
along the corridors: one day we may know
what brings about this ruthless alteration.

Soup and messages, sitting-up however hard,
more tough assignments gargling at the spoons,
'O-you-haven't-even-touched-your-lovely-flan!'

Of course not. What they eat is end
as grammar is uncoupled from their lives.

THE SECOND HUSBAND

He was a selfless man, beautiful
In all his actions if not handsome in
Himself—look through all his Orders, The Finn,
The Swede, The Turk; powers from Istanbul
To Christiana honoured him, a pin
To wear before the Emperor, a four-
starred crucifix, a jewelled watch the twin
Of Baron Swieten's—I keep them in a drawer.

Marrying him, I swam away from need.
The servants stopped their answering back, the bills
Arrived with presents; I discovered skills
I didn't know I had; the Court agreed
My figures for back pay; the last quadrilles
Sold first, those manuscripts I had to hand
He saw I wasn't cheated on; the quills
We never washed, the ink dried in its stand.

He was the most magnanimous of men,
One sign of it, I ceased my pregnancies.
Those days have long since gone; I have to please
New waves of pilgrims asking how and when.
My sister-in-law and I like two old trees
Live side by side; each plays the oracle.
Her mind is on those childhood prophecies,
Mine on the man who rescued me from hell.

And my misunderstood much-loved second
Husband wrote my first's biography:
I wondered at such generosity.
Now Europe listens, for the world is fecund
And everyone forgets reality
And praises the most marvellous of boys
Who drew the face of God for all to see
But was to me puerility and noise.

AT SCHUBERT'S GRAVE

They took their calipers and measured
        Dead Schubert's skull,
So Science was by Music pleasured,
        The void made null.

What could that space of fleshly tatters
        Say of its time,
Of keyboard lords and kindred matters
        Of the sublime?

The integers took up the story
        In fields of snow
And dreams through every category
        Were leased to go.

His was the head which notes had chosen
        To move within—
What gods and scientists had frozen
        Melted in him.

CARLOS SEIXAS, DYING

The quantity of pleasure-giving molecules
released into my brain by what I hear
inside my headset far exceeds the flow
from all arousal and orgasm
brought on by people, pictures, books and dreams.

You mean that you like music more than sex?

No, I hope for stars in order in my sky
and not chaotic suns. Nor is it Maths
which teem and follow from the brain's
eternal chemistry: here nothing good or bad
or true or false will ever be invented.

What follows when the music has to stop?

Post-aural sadness, no! Except, perhaps,
I see a well-dressed fashionable man
rising from the harpsichord and saying
to his wife, in current Portuguese,
he has too bad a headache to play on.

O worthless world, your small perfections showing!

CALIBAN v. PROSPERO

*(For the Sixtieth Birthday
of David Lumsdaine, composer)*

Wounds are healing in the night.
Westward, look the land is bright.
Caliban can touch his toes,
Cursing Prospero as he goes.

Sixty is a worthy age.
A robin redbreast in a cage
Is Heaven as it always was,
The Kingdom of Alas, Because.

And would you say of poor Ravel
Pardons him for writing well?
In 1815 Schubert wrote
More than half a million notes.

Death treads your lap with velvet paws
(It is the cause, my soul, the cause.)
The groans of tired Caliban
Complete the island's Five Year Plan.

Good art goes through sporadic slumps.
The Dean is dead, and what is trumps?
Sirs Mike and Harry and Lord B
Say don't take less than the CBE.

The currawongs' and magpies' cries
(Are there not Saints in holier skies?)
Give Orpheus his southern scale,
The flogger's whip, the harbour sail.

Calm seas and prosperous trips begin
(Alle meine Kraft is hin)
With Mother waving from the wharf
And genius, dry-eyed, heading North.

HISTORY

Friedrich Kutsky, known as 'Mac',
a lawyer's son who worked
with Russian military intelligence
and sent them warning England
wouldn't fight over Czechoslovakia,
was pushed off a grain freighter
in Lake Superior by an NKVD man
disguised as an elevator mechanic;
Manfred Löwenherz, 'Tom' to their circle
of University Marxists, helped organize
the destruction of the POUM
in Barcelona (Orwell had heard of
but never met him) and was himself
arrested in Moscow three weeks
after Catalonia surrendered: he is
presumed to have died in prison;
Frank Marshall, called 'The Englander'
because of his unlikely name, went
straight to Comintern Headquarters
and survived the show trials of '36
and '37, only to disappear from his flat
on the evening of the Molotov/Ribbentrop
Pact: his name is mentioned often
in the few authentic papers which
survive from Yezhov's office:
The Szymanowski brothers, Andrew
and Jerzy, led a Soviet expedition
to Zemyla and authenticated
the reports of nickel deposits—
both were murdered when their boat
was strafed by an unknown plane
on an expedition in Bering Strait:
the MVD uses more than ice-picks
was said in Moscow in 1940;
lastly Willy Marx, alias Oskar Odin,
'Old Grandad' to the group, jumped
in front of a Viennese tram the day
before the Anschluss, with plans for
Hitler's assassination in his shoes—
no one knows which Party organization
ordered his death. Six middle-class

66

boys from a racially-mixed Galician
town, three of them Jews, and only
one with a widow at a New England
College. Their story will not be told.

LE JARDIN SUSPENDU

Among the garçons edging the High Table
Of the Success Society were several pimply youths
Who never making prefect had a lot of yeast
In them; a funny thing, one older member said,
No matter what the Götterdämmerung,
How black and stiff each green initiative,
Some bunch of brazen never-readers
Turns up, shouting 'This is Now. This shift
Is What There Is and I am its Vizier.'
So much for tiredness and the vellum robing it,
So much for digits dripping down their columns,
For Third Worlds, Total Exclusion Zones
And bucklings of the plates of history—
A small moustache is working at the world
And won't be interrupted—you will hear it
When it croaks its beating need. Do you think
They knew they lived in an Age of Eloquence
Who were arguing with stars through fiery glass,
Who took perfection of the artist's form
For granted, working instead on how steam fell
And rose in tubes and how the ugly module
Of just seventy years might blaze a golden rose
For Demos? And in The Age of Epigram
When an out-of-kilter cummerbund
Or a wrong caesura in hexameters
Was most of what was worrying in art
Some brutal primitive was marketing
A colossal apparatus raising myth
To high symphonic shouting. No one
Can escape the garish present; it brings
You face to face with the Napoleon
In your mirror; your very nervous system
Is fundamentalist and knowing death
Instinctively it outlaws it,
Imagining committees to sit on
And hunting lodges still at planning stage,
A full obituary of accomplishments.
They raised their glasses then to fame and let
Those parvenus take up the light: the night
Was young, just like the world, and there was
Room in The Success Society for all.

In another part of town a curious band
Had come together, seemingly not talking,
Just looking at large folios of battered blue
And calling continuously for further drinks.
Someone named them to us, The Failure Society,
Pretty important people once whose books
Of hopelessness brought royalties flooding in,
Whose visits to mosquito coasts caused wars
Or burning of the staple crops. For years
They'd tinkered with the liturgy of hope,
Adapting social engineering to
The real face of evil, so they sat
At dinner parties on the host's right hand
And sauced the duller hates of millionaires
With rich lapsarian links: they didn't like it
When opponents asked them why the wickedness
Of worlds went hand in hand with personal
Success or what those prophets really meant
Who, choked on locusts and sand apparitions,
Called down the fire of heaven on Babylon
Or Rome or Rickmansworth. How wicked was it
To seek promotion in a PR firm
Or grow the largest marrow on the lot?
But now society had phased them out
And found it missed them—that tone, that dying fall,
That lyrical sussurus of despair
In novels or in sonnets lent relief
To people keen to learn a sense of style—
What could it be, that artful knowingness,
But the ancient acid of defeat, the sun
Which shone on tombs and Paradise alike?
So now behold the veterans convened
Again, as in the old days, swapping stories
Of why the Nobel Panel loved the dark
And where the flood of evil had its source.
They nominated one, a velvet bard
Too long in exile from extravagance,
To make the keynote speech. Tonight, he said,
I shall recall a golden age; I shan't
Speak of our exile in the provinces
Or how we washed the lavatories for Stocks
And Shares and ate the dead sea fruit of doubt.
My treatise is a poem, visionary
And full of an hermetic indolence;

69

To give it extra unction I shall make
Its title French, 'Le Jardin Suspendu'
Or 'Hanging Gardens' to the journalists —
As rich as *Salammbo*, as high above
The ordinary as *Sardanapalus*.
It covers death with that anticipation
We know as music when we lie awake
Chalked by the moon on bed and pillowslip —
Nothing of the vernacular will underpin
The picture, just a hocket of the desperate
Adding another note to consequence.

And he began. 'The king was sad and so
He ordered gods, not just his courtiers,
To raise a garden in the sky where plants
Might be the grander close to sun and rain
And standing tiptoe when the king approached
Would point him into heaven with a touch
Of leaf or stamen. A flying garden would
Have pleased him more, but this interpolation
Picked up the interstellar gossip so
The king could eavesdrop on the voices of
The dead, who told him men would not live long
But work much evil while they were on earth.
Saddened at this the king addressed himself
To welfare and the public good and works
Of art, to gates and roads and aqueducts:
He was not heard in heaven and the stars
Shone on regardless. If God could stoop, the king
Was told, He'd preen the smallest fly for fun.'

OXFORD POETS

Fleur Adcock
Edward Kamau Brathwaite
Joseph Brodsky
Basil Bunting
Daniela Crăsnaru
W. H. Davies
Michael Donaghy
Keith Douglas
D. J. Enright
Roy Fisher
David Gascoyne
Ivor Gurney
David Harsent
Gwen Harwood
Anthony Hecht
Zbigniew Herbert
Thomas Kinsella
Brad Leithauser
Derek Mahon

Medbh McGuckian
Jamie McKendrick
Sean O'Brien
Peter Porter
Craig Raine
Henry Reed
Christopher Reid
Stephen Romer
Carole Satyamurti
Peter Scupham
Penelope Shuttle
Louis Simpson
Anne Stevenson
George Szirtes
Grete Tartler
Edward Thomas
Charles Tomlinson
Chris Wallace-Crabbe
Hugo Williams